Contents

GW00866107

ame: _____

Draw over the broken lines to make four
spider threads. Start at the ☆.

2 Flowers in the garden

Draw over the broken lines to make a stalk for each flower.
Start at the ☆.

3 Blast-off!

Draw over the broken lines to show each rocket's take-off. Start at the ☆.

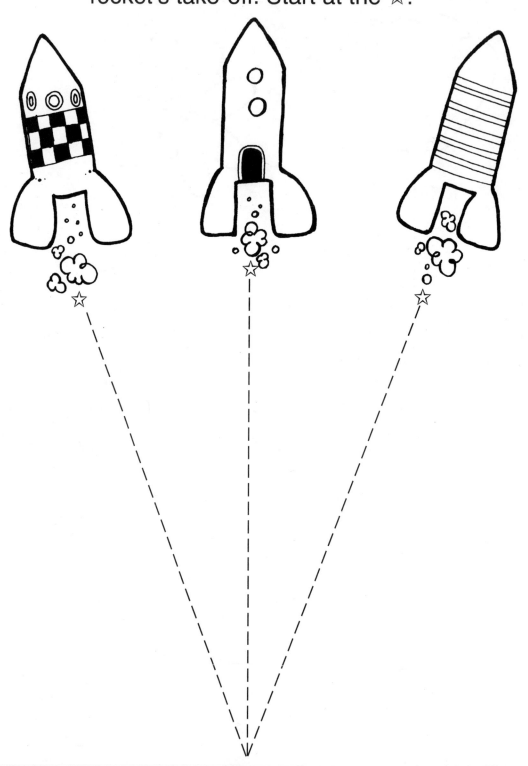

4 Don't look down!

Draw over the broken lines to make the ladder rungs, tightrope and balancing pole. Start at the ☆.

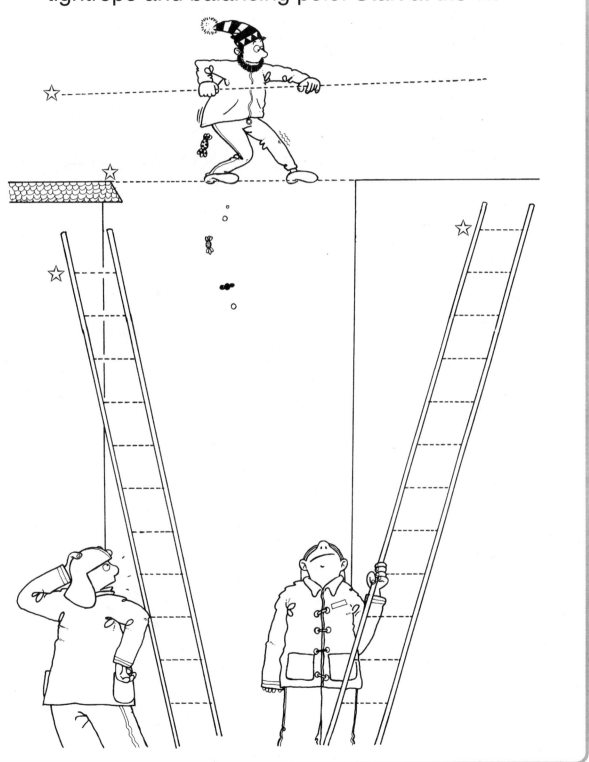

Draw over the broken lines in the blowers,
then colour them in. Start at the ☆.

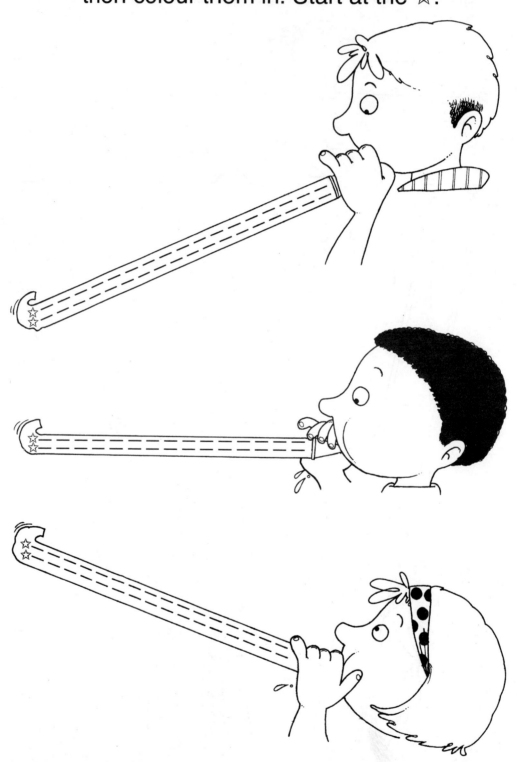

6 From outer space to Earth

Draw over the broken lines to show the spaceship's route to Earth. Start at the ☆.

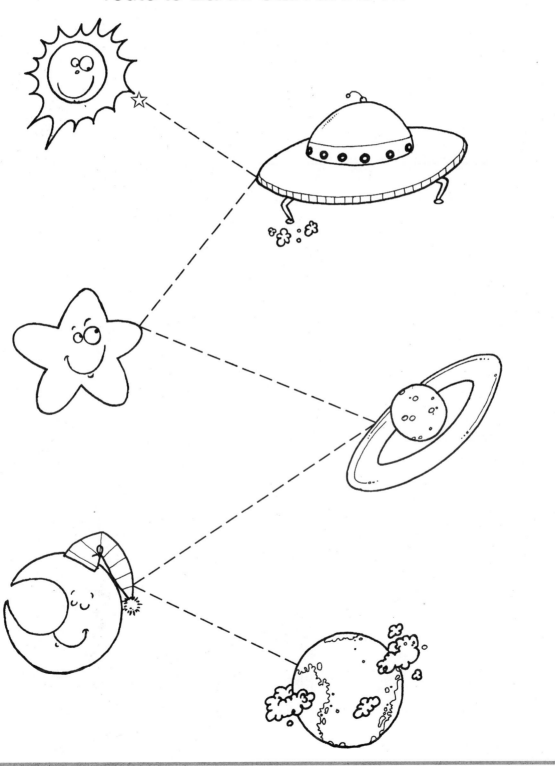

7 Practising patterns

Follow the arrows and draw over the broken lines to complete the patterns. Start at the ☆.

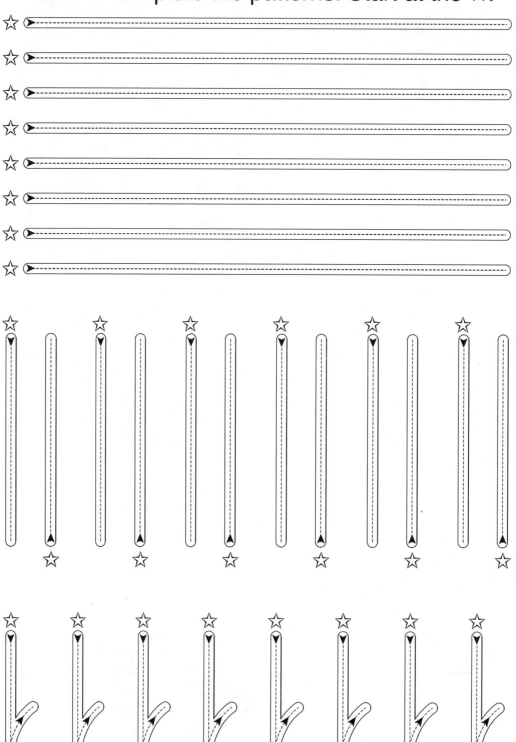

Follow the arrows and draw over the broken lines to complete the patterns. Start at the ☆.

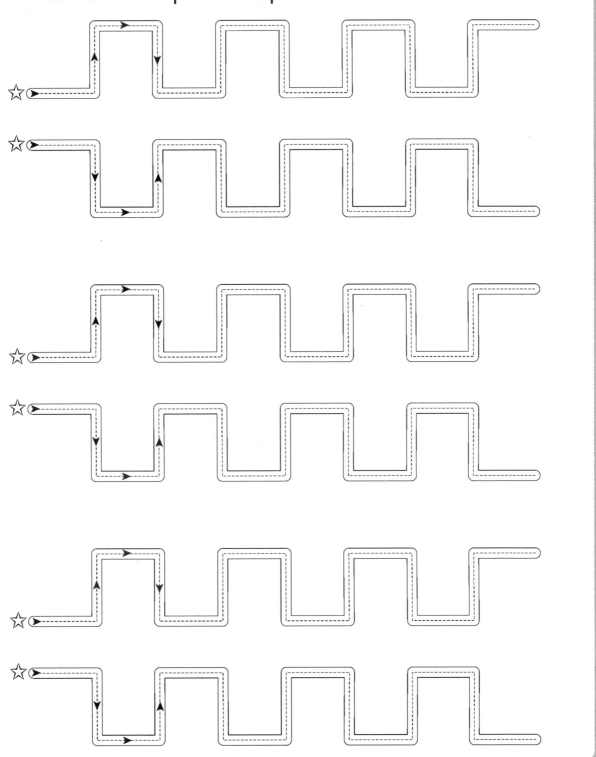

9 Practising patterns

Follow the arrows and draw over the broken lines to complete the patterns. Start at the ☆.

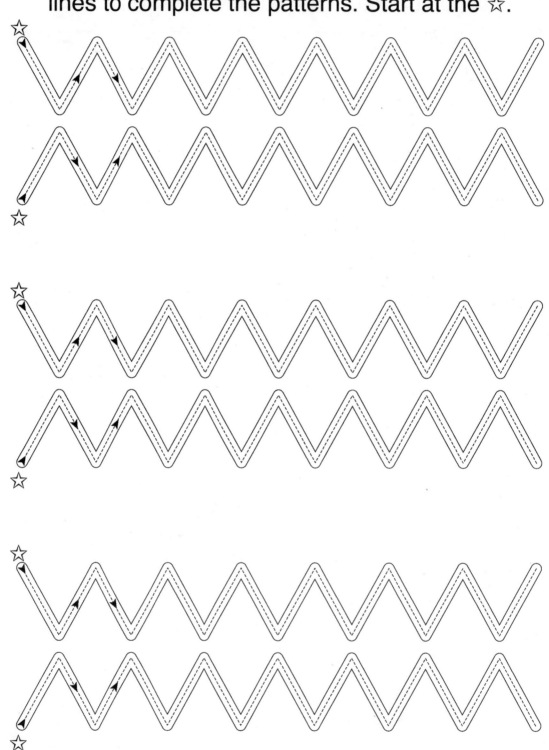

Hit the target!

Join the broken line from each arrow
to the target. Start at the ☆.

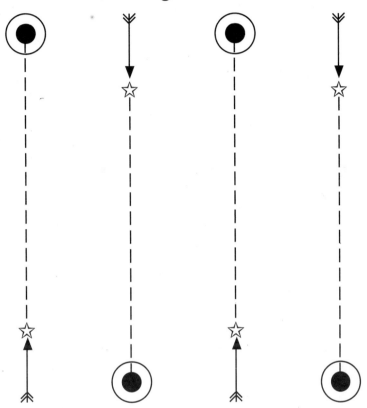

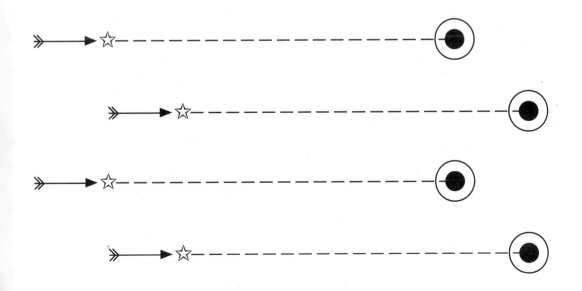

11 Hit the target!

Join the broken line from each arrow
to the target. Start at the ☆.

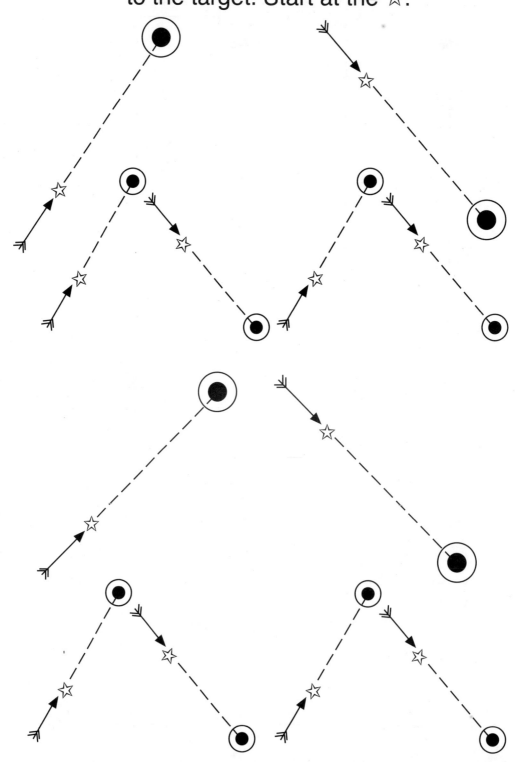

Follow the lines

Draw over the broken lines to make the shapes,
then colour them in. Follow the arrows. Start at the ☆.

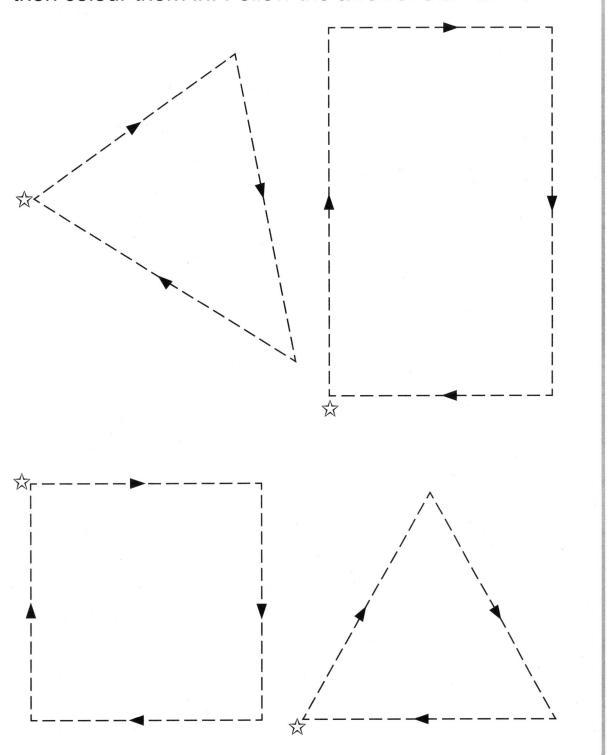

13 Practising patterns

Follow the arrows and draw over the broken lines to complete the patterns. Start at the ☆.

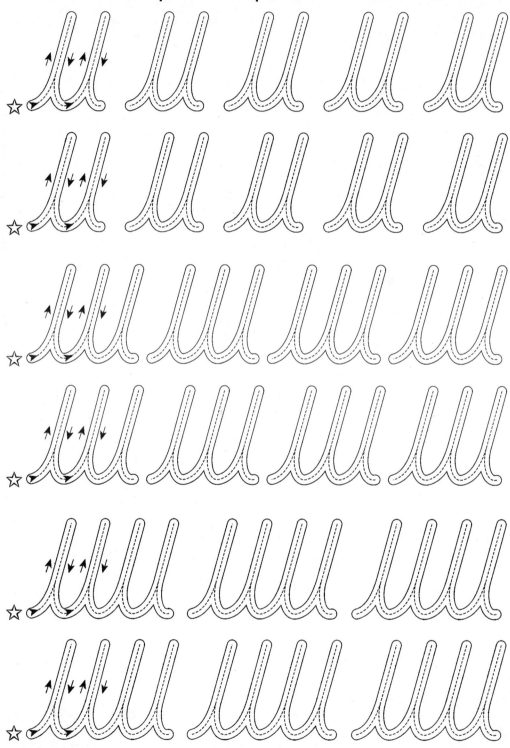

Practising patterns

Follow the arrows and draw over the broken lines to complete the patterns. Start at the ☆.

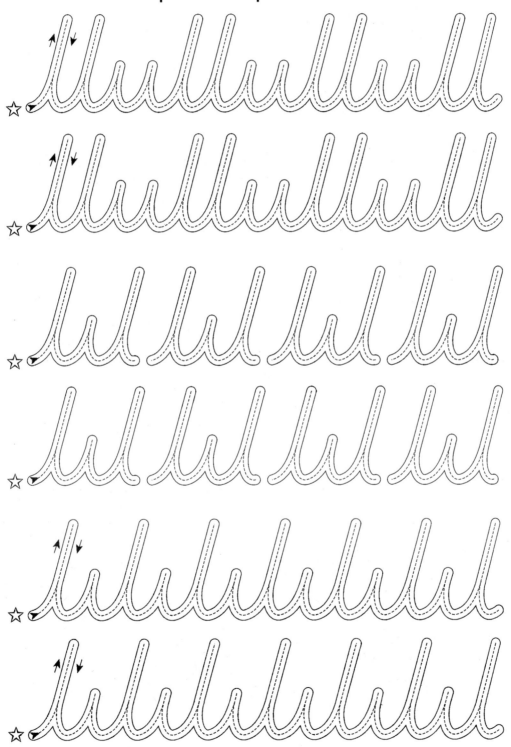

Touch the stars!

Draw over the broken lines to reach each
of the black stars. Start at the ☆.

16 Jump for it!

Draw over the broken line to show how the frog stays away from the hungry crocodiles and makes it to the other river bank. Start at the ☆.

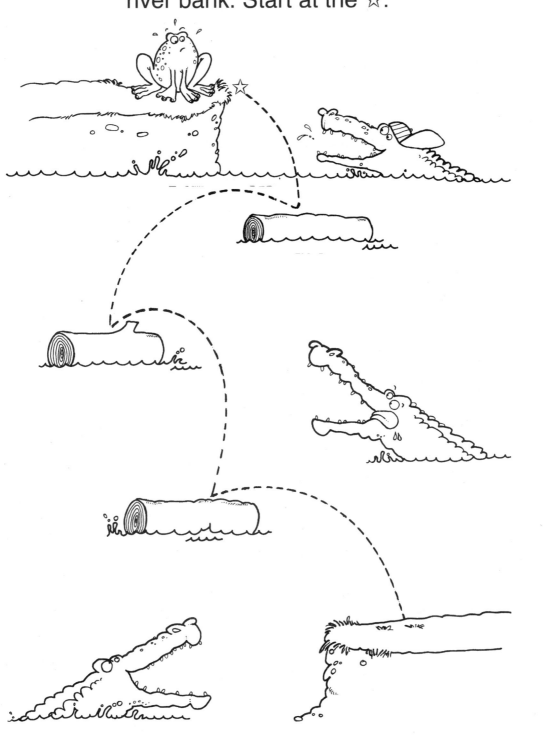

17 Bouncing balls

Draw over the broken lines to show how the four balls bounce. Start at the ☆.

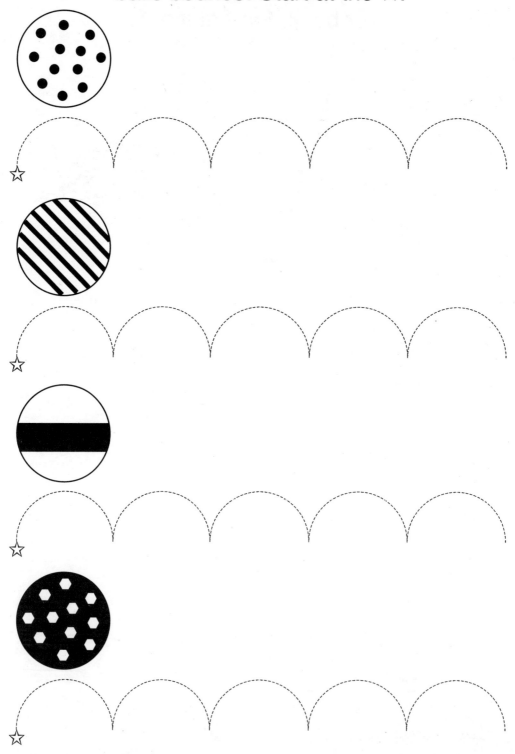

Draw over the broken lines to make three kite tails. Start at the ☆.

Draw over the broken line to show the route
the plane must take to stay away from the clouds.
Start at the ☆.

20 Practising patterns

Follow the arrows and draw over the broken
lines to complete the patterns. Start at the ☆.

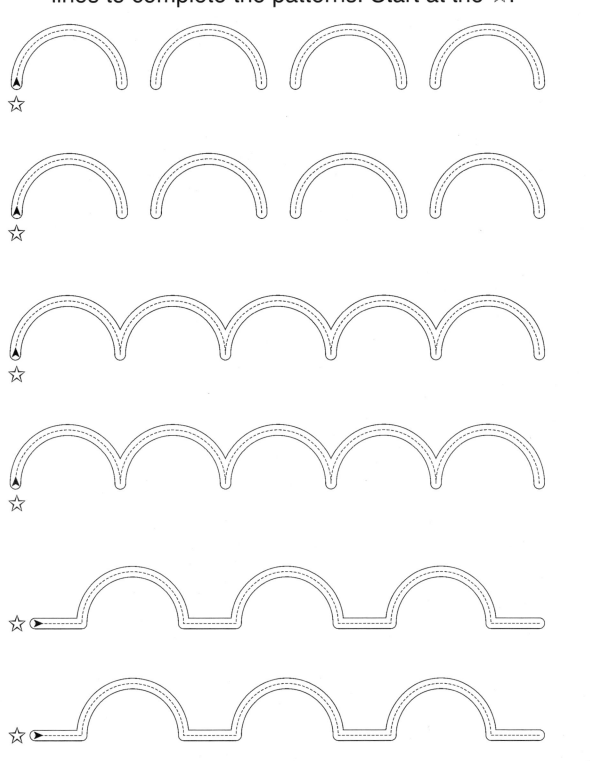

Practising patterns

Follow the arrows and draw over the broken lines to complete the patterns. Start at the ☆.

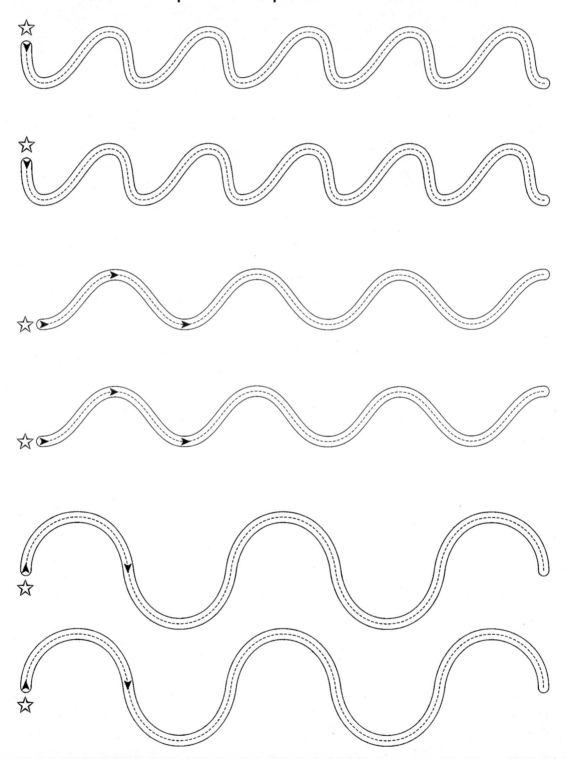

Follow the arrows and draw over the broken
lines to complete the circles. Then draw over the broken
circles to make a cuddly teddy bear. Start at the ☆.

23 Hit the target!

Join the broken line from each arrow
to the target. Start at the ☆.

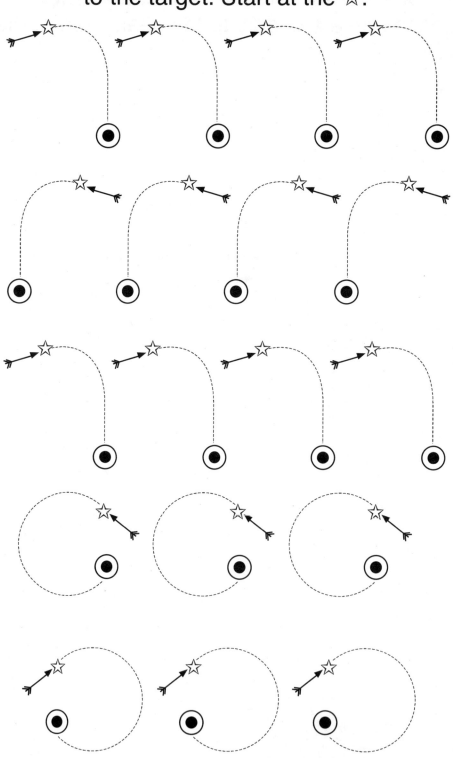

Draw over the broken lines to make five balls.
Colour the pattern in each ball. Start at the ☆.

Practising patterns

Follow the arrows and draw over the broken lines to complete the patterns. Start at the ☆.

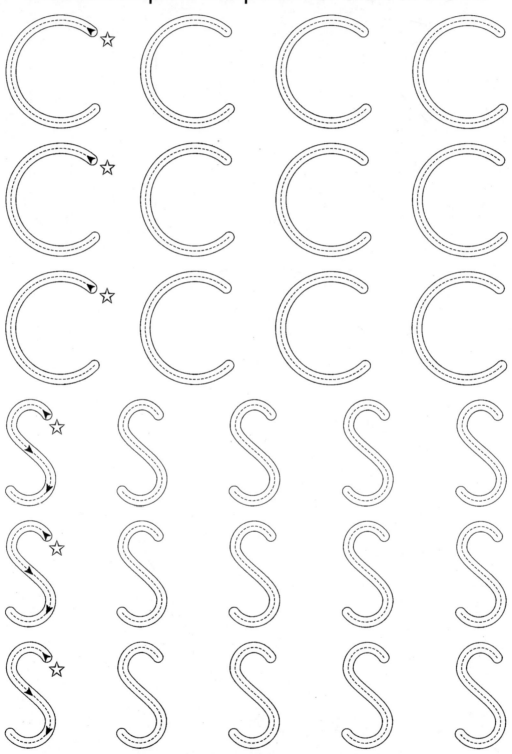

Follow the arrows and draw over the broken lines to complete the patterns. Start at the ☆.

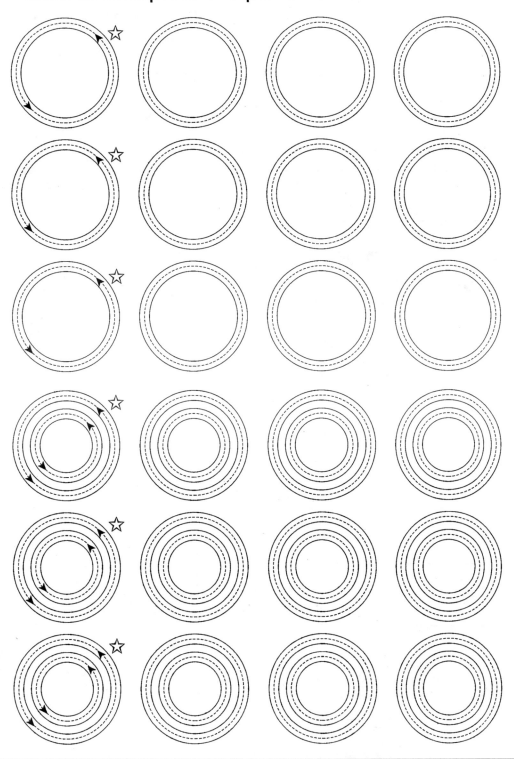

27 Follow the lines

Draw over the broken lines to make a house,
then colour in each shape. Make sure the
same shapes are the same colour. Start at the ☆.

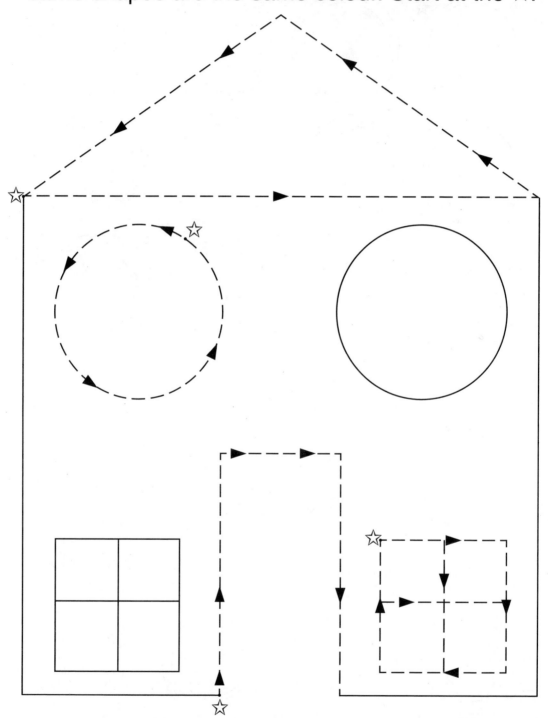

28 Join the lines

Draw over the broken lines to make a yacht
and an aircraft. Follow the numbers and arrows.
Start at the ☆.

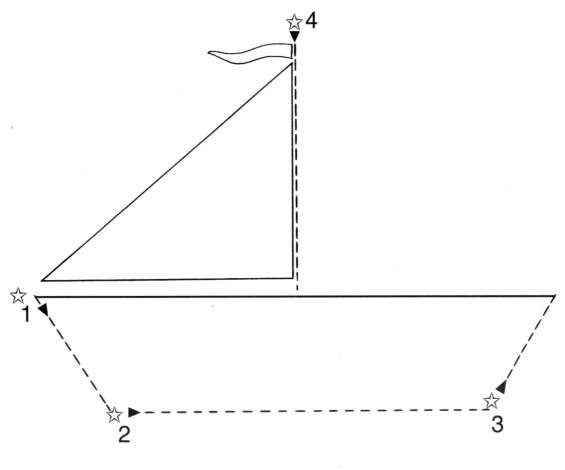

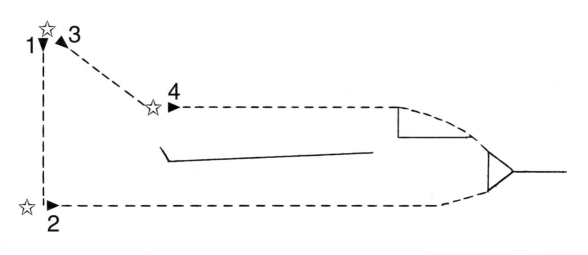

29 Join the lines

Draw over the broken lines to make a car
and a tractor.

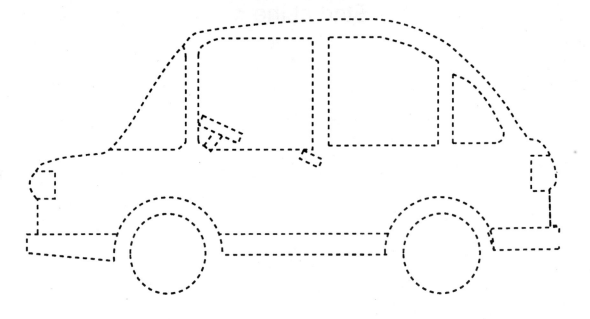

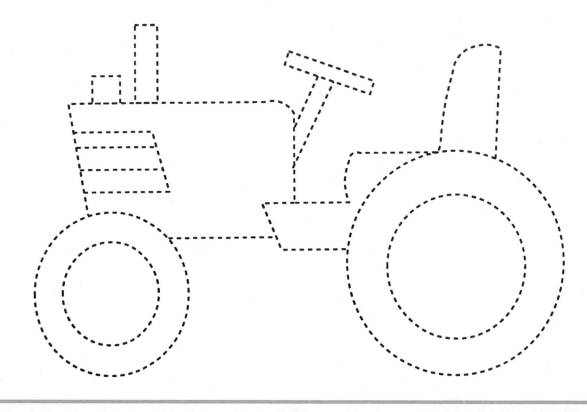

Join the lines

Draw over the broken lines to make a train and a bus.

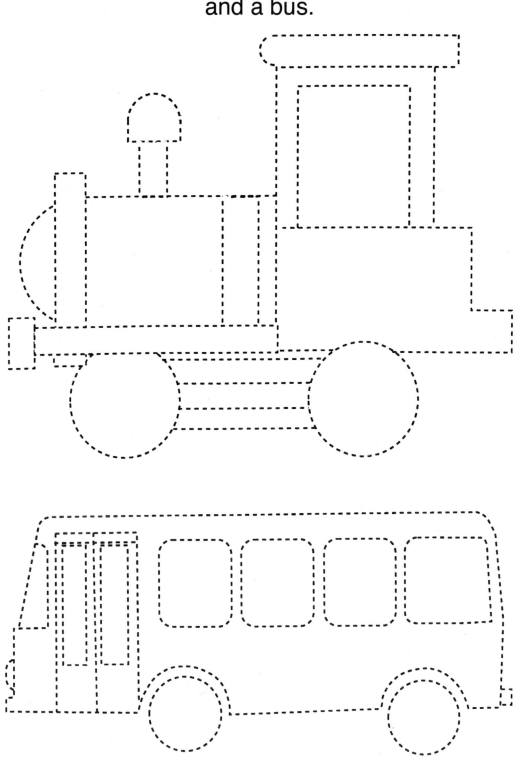

Monkey business

Draw over the broken lines to make five long monkey tails.
Start at the ☆.

32 Practising patterns

Follow the arrows and draw over the broken lines to complete the patterns. Start at the ☆.

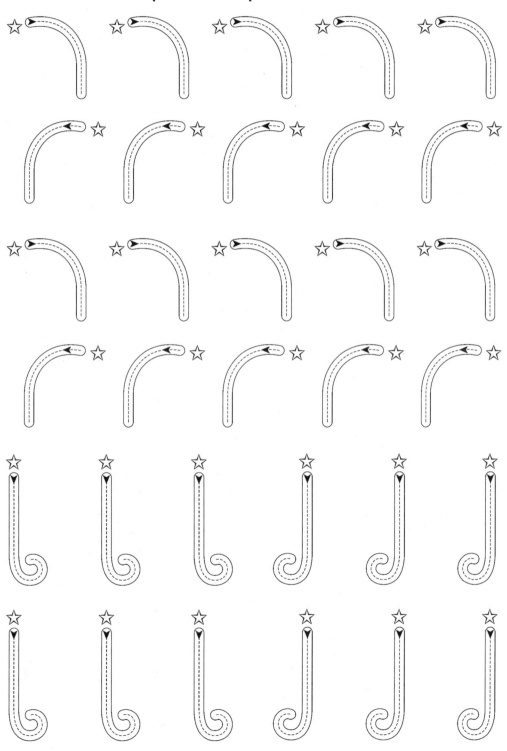

33 Practising patterns

Follow the arrows and draw over the broken lines to complete the patterns. Start at the ☆.

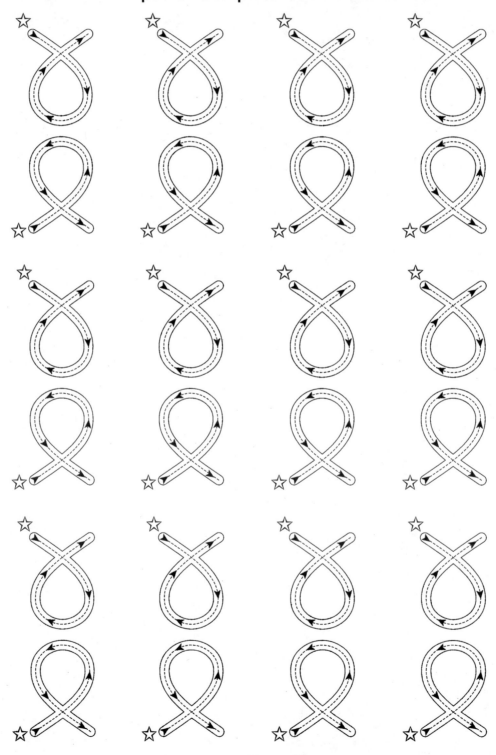

34) Practising patterns

Follow the arrows and draw over the broken lines to complete the patterns. Start at the ☆.

Join the broken line from each arrow to the target. Start at the ☆.

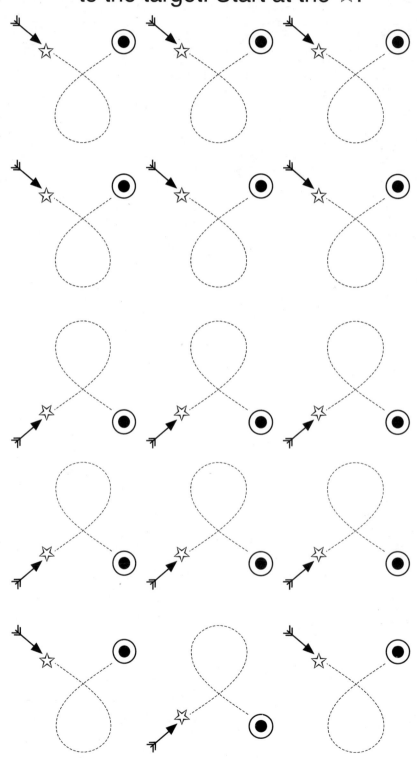

Follow the arrows and draw over the broken lines to complete the patterns. Start at the ☆.

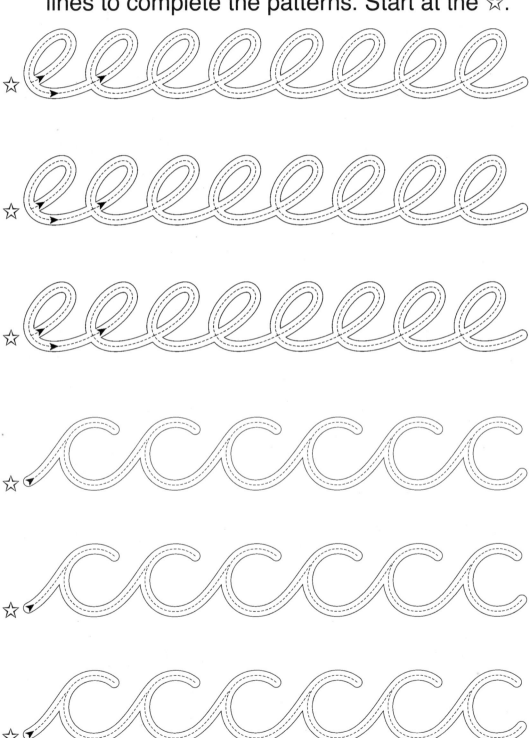

37 Practising patterns

Follow the arrows and draw over the broken lines to complete the patterns. Start at the ☆.

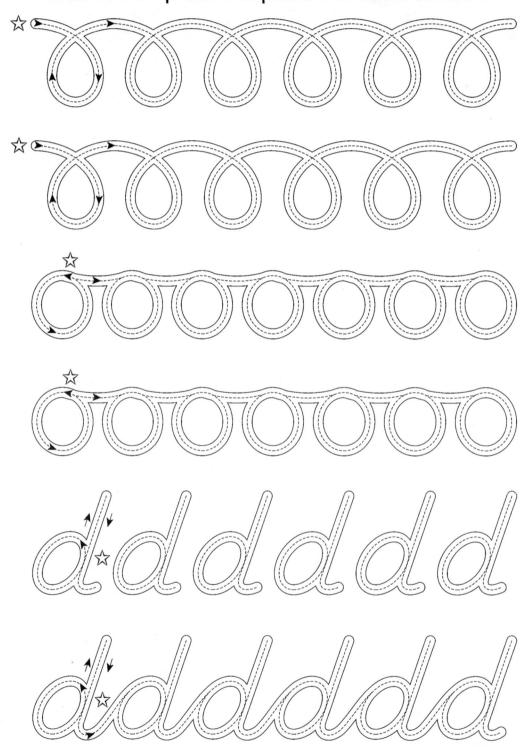

Join the lines

Draw over the broken line from each arrow
to its target. Follow the numbers. Start at the ☆.

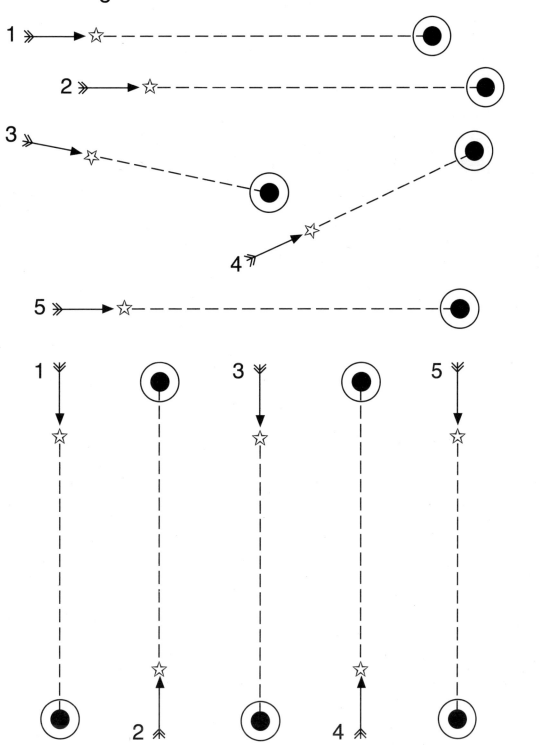

Join the lines

Draw over the broken lines to complete the shapes. Follow the arrows. Start at the ☆.

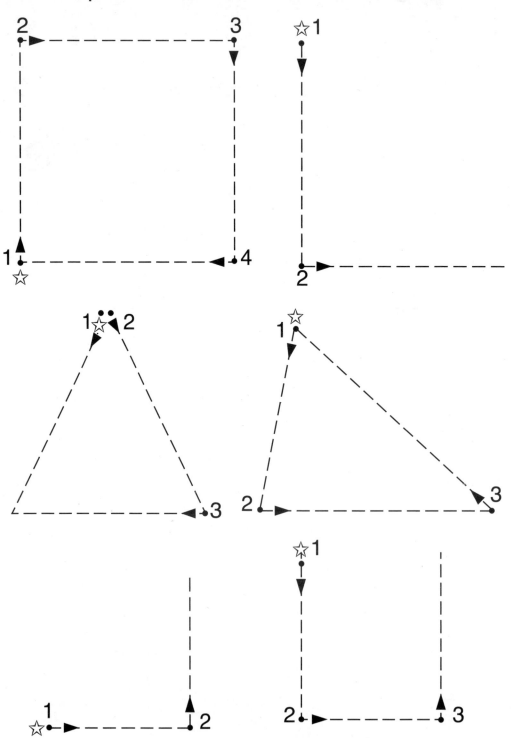

40 Hit the target!

Join the broken line from each arrow
to the target. Start at the ☆.

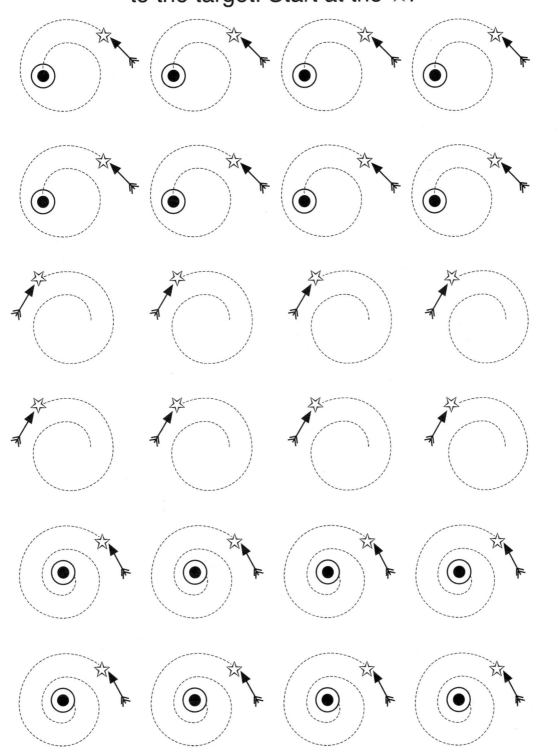

41 Draw your own patterns

Draw over the broken lines on the first fish to make a pattern. Start at the ☆. Then draw different patterns on the other fish.

42 Draw your own patterns

Draw over the broken lines to make a pattern on the first caterpillar. Start at the ☆. Then draw different patterns on the other caterpillars.

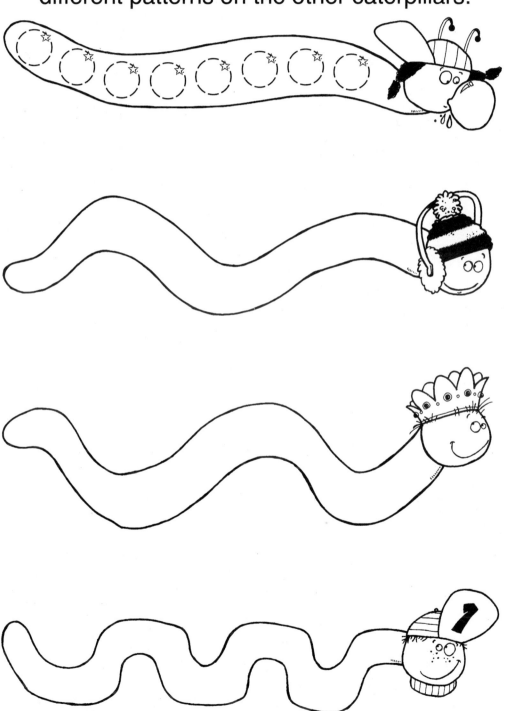

43 Join the lines

Draw over the broken lines to make letter shapes.
Follow the arrows. Start at the ☆.

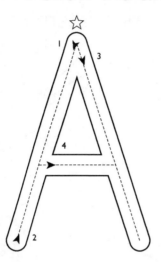

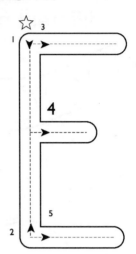

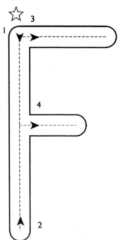

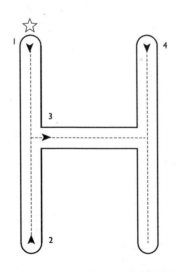

Draw over the broken lines to make letter shapes.
Follow the arrows. Start at the ☆.

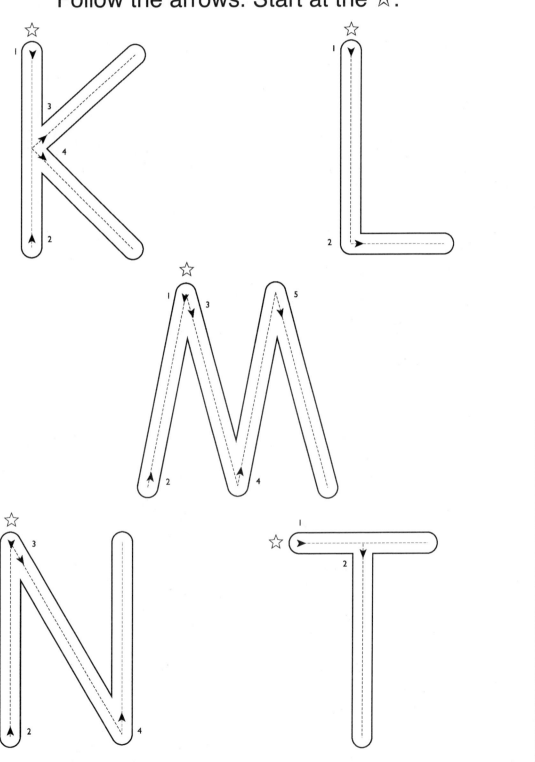

45 Join the lines

Draw over the broken lines to make letter shapes.
Follow the arrows. Start at the ☆.

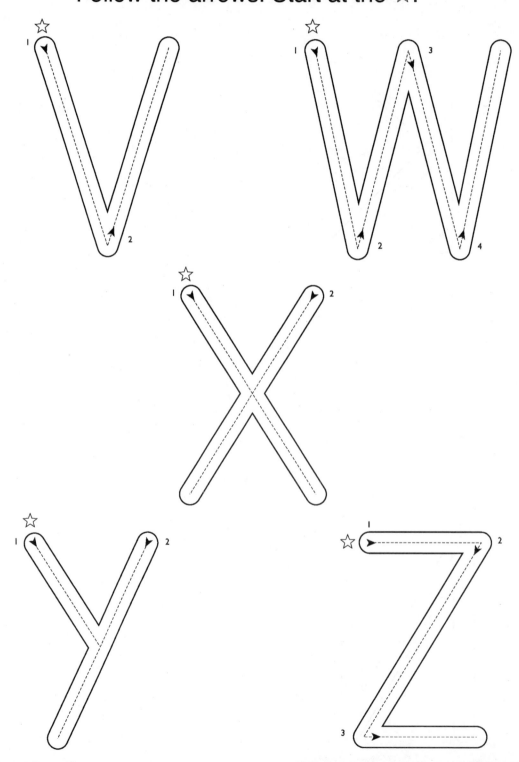

46

Join the lines

Draw over the broken lines to make letter shapes.
Follow the arrows. Start at the ☆.

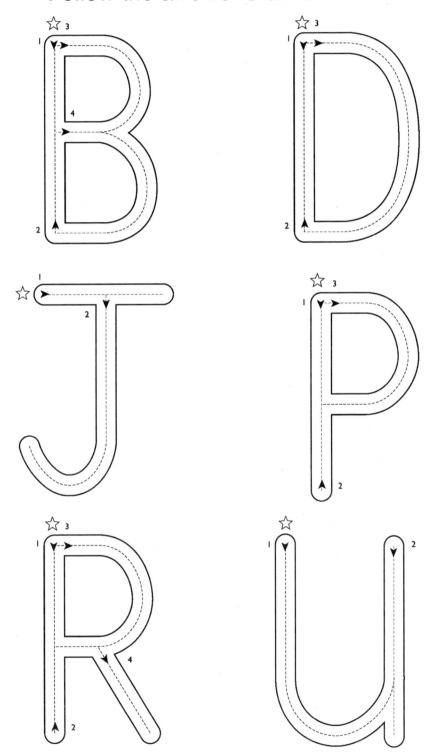

47 Join the lines

Draw over the broken lines to make letter shapes.
Follow the arrows. Start at the ☆.

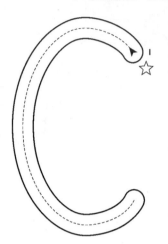

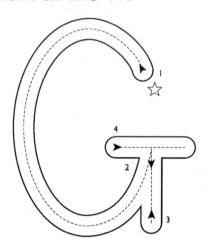

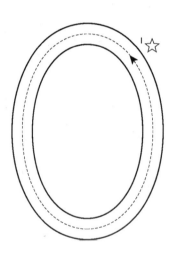

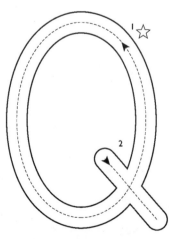

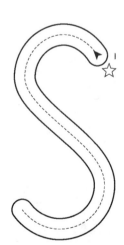